FULL OF PROMISE

8 INTERACTIVE BIBLE STUDIES FOR
SMALL GROUPS AND INDIVIDUALS

BRYSON SMITH
AND PHIL CAMPBELL

matthiasmedia

Full of Promise
Second edition
© Matthias Media 2011

First published 1997

Matthias Media
(St Matthias Press Ltd ACN 067 558 365)
PO Box 225
Kingsford NSW 2032
Australia
Telephone: (02) 9233 4627; international: +61 2 9233 4627
Email: info@matthiasmedia.com.au
Internet: www.matthiasmedia.com.au

Matthias Media (USA)
Telephone: 330 953 1702; international: +1 330 953 1702
Email: sales@matthiasmedia.com
Internet: www.matthiasmedia.com

ISBN 978 1 921441 89 9

Cover design and typesetting by Matthias Media.
Series concept designs by Lankshear Design.

›› CONTENTS

» HOW TO MAKE THE MOST OF THESE STUDIES

1. What is an Interactive Bible Study?

Interactive Bible Studies are a bit like a guided tour of a famous city. They take you through a particular part of the Bible, helping you to know where to start, pointing out things along the way, suggesting avenues for further exploration, and making sure that you know how to get home. Like any good tour, the real purpose is to allow you to go exploring for yourself—to dive in, have a good look around, and discover for yourself the riches that God's word has in store.

In other words, these studies aim to provide stimulation and input and point you in the right direction, while leaving you to do plenty of the exploration and discovery yourself.

We hope that these studies will stimulate lots of 'interaction'—interaction with the Bible, with the things we've written, with your own current thoughts and attitudes, with other people as you discuss them, and with God as you talk to him about it all.

2. The format

The studies contain four main components:
- sections of text that introduce, inform, summarize and challenge
- numbered questions that help you examine the passage and think through its meaning
- 'Implications' sections that help you think about what this passage means for you and your life today
- suggestions for thanksgiving and prayer as you close.

3. How to use these studies on your own

- Before you begin, pray that God would open your eyes to what he is saying in the Bible, and give you the spiritual strength to do something about it.
- Work through the study, reading the text, answering the questions about the Bible passage, and exploring things in more detail as you have time.
- Resist the temptation to skip over the 'Implications' and 'Give thanks and pray' sections at the end. It is important that we not only hear and understand God's word, but also respond to it. These closing sections help us do that.
- Take what opportunities you can to talk to others about what you've learnt.

4. How to use these studies in a small group

- Much of the above applies to group study as well. The studies are suitable for structured Bible study or cell groups, as well as for more informal pairs and triplets. Get together with a friend or friends and work through them at your own pace; use them as the basis for regular Bible study with your spouse. You don't need the formal structure of a 'group' to gain maximum benefit.

- For small groups, it is *very useful* if group members can work through the study themselves *before* the group meets. The group discussion can take place comfortably in an hour (depending on how sidetracked you get!) if all the members have done some work in advance.
- The role of the group leader is to direct the course of the discussion and to try to draw the threads together at the end. If you are a group leader, the material in the appendix 'Tips for leaders' will help you think through how to use these studies in a group setting.
- If your group members usually don't work through the study in advance, it's extra important that the leader prepares which parts to concentrate on, and which parts to glide past more quickly. In particular, the leader will need to select which of the 'Implications' to focus on.
- We haven't included an 'answer guide' to the questions in the studies. This is a deliberate move. We want to give you a guided tour of the Bible, not a lecture. There is more than enough in the text we have written and the questions we have asked to point you in what we think is the right direction. The rest is up to you.

5. Bible translation

Previous editions of this Interactive Bible Study have assumed that most readers would be using the New International Version of the Bible. However, since the release of the English Standard Version in 2001, many have switched to the ESV for study purposes. So with this new edition of *Full of Promise*, we have decided to quote from and refer to the ESV text, which we recommend.

WHEN GOOD TURNS BAD

[GENESIS 1-11]

1. Without looking at a Bible, draw a diagram or a timeline containing what you see as the main events of the Old Testament.

The big picture

JIGSAW PUZZLES ARE GREAT FUN. At least that's what people keep telling me. Personally, I find them hard work. Sitting at a table surrounded by hundreds of little pieces of coloured cardboard only confuses and frustrates me.

The way I feel about jigsaw puzzles is the way many of us feel about the Old Testament. We may know lots of individual stories of the Old Testament, like Daniel in the lion's den or David and Goliath, but we're not really sure how they all fit together. In fact, some of us may not even know that they do fit together! The end result is that the Old Testament can be a confusing and frustrating part of the Bible, which we either avoid altogether or dip into at random like a phone book or a dictionary.

The aim of these studies is to take some of the confusion out of the Old Testament by providing an overview of its main themes and events. The studies will be like taking a scenic flight over a spectacular but varied landscape. From the plane we'll be able to see the main points of interest—but naturally, we won't have the time to land and study many things in detail.

By the time our flight is over, however, we will have gained an appreciation of the overall landscape, and how it all fits together. That's a particularly important thing to do with the Old Testament, because the events of this part of the Bible prepare us for the greatest event in the history of this planet: the life, death and resurrection of Jesus Christ.

The big question is: where do we start? There are so many different people, places and events. Which should we look at first? Well, believe it or not, when it comes to the Old Testament, the best place to start is at the beginning.

Read Genesis 1:1–2:3.

2. Do you notice any recurring words or phrases?

3. What do you think these patterns tell us about God and the world?

4. What things reflect the fact that humanity has a special place in God's plans?

A good creation

WE HAVE DISCOVERED THAT THE OLD Testament opens with God creating a good world. We have also discovered that God is a powerful and systematic creator. First he separates all the different compartments of creation, and then he methodically fills each compartment with appropriate things. For example, first the land and water are separated, and then the water is filled with sea creatures and the land is filled with vegetation and animals.

Genesis reveals a creator who has a place for everything, and who puts everything in its place. This world has a design and purpose. We are not here by accident!

Within God's design for creation, humanity has a central role. Man is created to be God's representative on earth, placed here to enjoy fellowship with God and care for his creation. In this respect, God's creative work culminates in the 'rest' of the seventh day. The seventh day is a picture of God and humanity enjoying perfect rest together in an unspoiled world.

Read Genesis 3.

5. Genesis 3 records the rebellion of Adam and Eve against God's rule. This is often called 'the Fall'. How is the Fall typical of all sin (3:1-7)?

6. In Genesis 3:8-24, God punishes Adam and Eve for their rebellion. Things have changed. How is the created order now different?

A bad decision

AS THE STORY OF GENESIS UNFOLDS, God's good creation is tainted by sin. In Genesis 3, Adam and Eve take life into their own hands and, instead of following God's good instructions, they make up their own rules and decide to eat from the tree of the knowledge of good and evil. This rebellious act immediately introduces tension, mistrust, and antagonism into all levels of what was a good creation.

Mankind is now engaged in a struggle with nature. Man and woman are now engaged in a struggle with each other. Even at one of humanity's most beautiful and treasured moments—the birth of a child—there is now pain and anguish. All because humans thought they knew better than God.

And the bad news is only just beginning.

Skim read Genesis 4–11.

7. Note the main events of chapters 4-11. How do they demonstrate the spread of sin and the worsening of creation?

8. Despite all the bad things that happen in these chapters, what evidence is there of God still actively blessing his creation?

The spread of sin

WE'RE ONLY 11 CHAPTERS INTO THE Old Testament but already things seem to be going from bad to worse. Things started out so well: God, mankind and nature were in harmony within a good creation. But before long the whole world unravels into murder, incest, violence, deceit and corruption. Indeed, by the time you reach the end of chapter 11, you'd be excused for wondering why God bothers!

Despite this escalation of sin and evil in the world, there are still signs that God is at work blessing his creation and trying to rectify things. For example, even in the midst of judging sin by means of the flood, God graciously rescues one man and his family. God even blesses Noah with words very similar to those he spoke to Adam and Eve (Gen 9:1-3). What we are seeing is God's unwavering commitment to his creation. Even when mankind is repeatedly unfaithful, God keeps faithfully working to reverse the effects of the Fall.

This is an exciting discovery about God for, as we will see, it leads us straight to Jesus Christ.

» **Implications**

(Choose one or more of the following to think about further or to discuss in your group.)

- Genesis describes God as a powerful and loving creator. Look up the following passages and consider how this truth should shape our lives.

  - Psalm 104

  - Luke 12:22-34

- "I believe that God is nature—God is the living earth. That's why we should look after our environment." How would you respond to that comment?

- In Romans 1:20 we are told that creation testifies to certain things about God. What can we tell about God from creation? Which areas of creation help you personally to appreciate God's greatness?

- Because of the Fall, life in the world is a mixture of good and bad, achievement and frustration. In what specific areas of life are you feeling this?

- From the following passages, what was Jesus Christ's role in creation? How should this affect the way we respond to Christ?

  - John 1:1-3

  - Colossians 1:15-17

  - Hebrews 1:1-4

- On a scale of 1-10 (10 being the highest), how would you rate God's faithfulness to his creation? Mark your rating on the scale below.

1   2   3   4   5   6   7   8   9   10

- From what you've seen so far, how would you rate mankind's faithfulness to God?

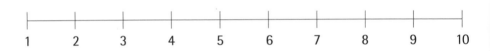

1	2	3	4	5	6	7	8	9	10

» Give thanks and pray

- Thank God for his specific design and purpose in creation, and thank him for the precious gift of life that we so often take for granted.
- Ask God to forgive you for the times when you have followed in the footsteps of Adam and Eve, trying to rule your own life and disobeying God's word.
- Give thanks for Jesus, the Word, through whom all things were made.

PROMISES, PROMISES

[GENESIS 12–50]

1. A television reporter stops you in the street to ask for your opinion on what's wrong with this world. How do you answer?

A new start

"**D**O WE RENOVATE OR DEMOL-ish?" It's a question hundreds of home owners ask themselves each year. Do we improve the kitchen, update the bathroom and add a couple of extra rooms? Or is it easier to just pull the whole house down and build a completely new one? Do we renovate or demolish?

In Genesis 9-11, that's the question God has been asking about his creation.

We've discovered that the Old Testament started out well. In Genesis 1, God made a good creation in which he, humanity and nature all related harmoniously. But mankind rebelled against God's rule and, as a result, creation spiralled into a cycle of sin and punishment. God responded by almost demolishing the world and making a new start with Noah. And yet by the time we reach the tower of Babel (Genesis 11), humanity has again degenerated into an arrogant, self-assertive community that attempts to force its way into heaven itself! The rot runs very, very deep.

So what is God to do? Is there a workable way to renovate creation, or should he demolish his world once and for all? Can humanity be repaired? Or is it simply better to destroy absolutely everything and start again? Let's see what God decides.

Read Genesis 12:1-9.

2. What does God promise Abram in these verses?

3. Compare Genesis 12:2 with Genesis 11:4. What do these verses tell us about humanity and God?

Read Genesis 15:1-6.

4. God repeats his promises to Abram. What new things do we discover about God and Abram in these verses?

5. How do God's promises to Abram reflect a return to the good creation of Genesis 1-2?

Eden revisited

REMARKABLY, SURPRISINGLY, GRA-ciously, God chooses to repair the sin in creation by means of certain promises to Abram. Specifically, God promises three things:

i. God promises that Abram's descendants will increase and become a great nation. To reflect this promise, God changes Abram's name to Abraham (which means 'father of a multitude').

ii. God promises to give Abraham's descendants their own special land.

iii. God promises to bless Abraham's descendants, and promises that they in turn will bring blessing to all people.

God's promises to Abraham are majestic acts of grace, because through them God is committing himself to reversing the effects of the Fall. Just as God created Adam and Eve, placed them in a special land and blessed them, he now promises to create a new people whom he will also put in a special land and bless. Through his promises to Abraham, God is vowing to bring into existence a new humanity in which the curses of the Fall will be replaced with blessing.

6. The remainder of Genesis details the next few generations of Abraham's family, finishing with the story of Joseph. Skim through your Bible and note down some of the main events in these chapters. As you do, draw a family tree from Abraham to Joseph.

Main events	Family tree

7. How do the events in these chapters relate to God's promises to Abraham?

8. Read Joseph's last words (Gen 50:24-25). How does Genesis end in relation to God's promises?

Abraham and the rest of the Old Testament

GOD'S PROMISES TO ABRAHAM ARE very important in the Bible. They are promises to undo the effects of the Fall. They are promises to renovate the world and take life back to a garden-of-Eden experience. They are also promises that form the backbone of the rest of the Old Testament. Everything that happens in the Old Testament from Genesis 12 onwards has God's promises to Abraham in view. That is essentially what we're going to discover in the remainder of these studies. In every study we will see God working to fulfil his promises to Abraham. The great tragedy, however, is that in every study we will also see how mankind's unfaithfulness keeps working against God's desire to reverse the Fall.

Abraham, Jesus and us

THE MOST EXCITING THING ABOUT the Old Testament is that it prepares us for Jesus Christ. Time and time again throughout these studies, we will discover ways in which the Old Testament points forward to the coming of Christ. This is especially the case with God's promises to Abraham.

The New Testament depicts Jesus Christ as the ultimate fulfilment of all of God's promises (2 Cor 1:20). God's promises to Abraham are no exception. Christ brings into existence a people of God who have a special inheritance that will not fade, and who have been blessed with every spiritual blessing. In so doing, Jesus Christ is the one who reverses the Fall and fulfils God's promises to Abraham.

» Implications

(Choose one or more of the following to think about further or to discuss in your group.)

- Abraham is considered an important person in the New Testament as well as the Old. Look up the following passages and consider how Abraham helps us to better understand how we are saved by Christ.

  - Romans 4

  - Hebrews 11:8-12

  - Galatians 4:21-31 (for the adventurous)

- We, like Abraham, are saved by trust in God's promises. This is quite a surprising way to be saved. What are some other ways that people think they can be put right with God?

- When is it hard to trust God?

- What things can we do to strengthen our trust in God? Be specific.

- "God doesn't care about the world. If he did, he would have done something about all the evil things that happen." How would you respond to this comment?

- We've now reached the end of Genesis. Again, give God's faithfulness a rating from 1-10.

- Abraham and his descendants are now the focal point of God's dealings with mankind. From what you've seen in this study, give them a score for their faithfulness to God.

» Give thanks and pray

- Thank God that we are saved through faith in his promises and in the Son he sent to fulfil them. Praise God's trustworthy and faithful nature.
- Repent of your own unfaithfulness to God.
- Ask for God's help in bringing all your worries, fears and concerns to him, and in wholly trusting his good promises.

THE GREAT ESCAPE

[EXODUS–DEUTERONOMY]

1. Using no more than three sentences, write a summary of the book of Genesis.

Escapes and rescue missions

As Ross McGill lay recovering in hospital, surrounded by TV cameras, the eyes of the nation were on him. He was a survivor. More than that—he was a hero. After the helicopter he was in crashed in a dry creek bed, Ross dragged himself on his hands and knees through the remote Australian desert for over 12 hours to raise the alarm and save his friends. It was a dramatic rescue. It was a great escape, against incredible odds. Don't you just love stories like that?

If you enjoy escape stories then you're going to love this study, because we've reached the greatest escape of the Old Testament.

The escape is called 'the Exodus', and through it God rescues over 600,000 people from slavery and oppression in a display of awesome power. But it's not just the scale of the escape that makes the Exodus so significant. The Exodus is critically important to what happens in the rest of the Old Testament. If we don't understand the Exodus then there is much in the Bible that we won't fully appreciate, including the death and resurrection of Jesus Christ.

By the end of Genesis, Joseph (Abraham's great grandson) had become a man of great power in Egypt. Through Joseph's influence, all of Abraham's descendants had settled in Egypt so as to survive a severe famine. The book of Exodus records the events following Joseph's time.

2. Read Exodus 1:6-12. What parts of God's promises to Abraham do you see being fulfilled?

3. Abraham's descendants, the Israelites, are persecuted by Pharaoh and subjected to slavery. Read Exodus 2:23-24 and 3:15-17. What does God plan to do and why?

4. Pharaoh refuses to let Israel free despite numerous plagues sent by God. God sends one last terrible plague. Quickly skim read Exodus 12:1-41. What eventually forced Pharaoh to let Israel go?

The birth of a nation

THE BOOK OF EXODUS OPENS WITH things not looking too good for Abraham's descendants. The Israelites have indeed become very numerous, but there still seems a long way to go before God's promises to Abraham are fulfilled. In particular, the people of Israel aren't really galvanized into a nation yet. That's why the Exodus is such an important event.

In the Exodus, God begins to fulfil his promise to Abraham by forming Israel into a unified, distinct nation that is on its way to the Promised Land. The Exodus marks the start of the Jewish nation—and throughout its history, the Exodus was to be Israel's reference point for everything. To be a Jew meant to identify yourself with this escape. That's why the Exodus was to mark the start of the Jewish calendar (Exod 12:2).

As well as showing that the Exodus is the start of the Israelite nation, the Bible also emphasizes certain characteristics of the way the Israelites were rescued.

- **A lamb is sacrificed**
  When God saw the blood of the sacrificed lamb on an Israelite door, he passed over the house. The death of that innocent lamb took the place of the death of the Israelites' own first-born.

- **God did it**
  National Israel did not come into existence because it achieved its own victory. It's not that Israel waged war against Egypt and eventually won its freedom. Israel was released because God did it!

- **From slavery to freedom**
  Israel had been oppressed and enslaved in Egypt, and now it was free. God heard Israel's cry, and remembered his promises. He freed the nation. Slavery was gone.

- **From poverty to riches**
  The Exodus meant going from poverty to riches. It wasn't as if the Israelites only managed to get out with the clothes on their backs. They walked away with the treasures of Egypt in their suitcases. And the Egyptians even handed them over voluntarily!

On any terms, this is an incredible escape. Through the sacrificial death of a lamb, God took his people from slavery and poverty to freedom and great riches. It is the greatest escape of the Old Testament. But it is not the greatest escape of the Bible—there's one other escape in the Bible that's even more phenomenal. But more of that later. Let's first see what happens to Israel now that they have been set free.

5. Read Exodus 19:1-8. After freeing the people of Israel from their oppression, God gathers them together at Mount Sinai and explains his plans for their future. What is God going to do with Israel and how do these plans relate to his promises to Abraham?

6. What do the Israelites say they'll do?

7. Read Exodus 16:1-3, 17:1-2 and 32:1-4. Despite what they said, has the Israelites' behaviour improved?

8. Skim quickly through the contents of Exodus 24-40. What do these chapters seem to be mainly about? Why do you think this receives so much attention?

9. How does the book of Exodus end (40:34-38)? How does this ending relate to God's promises to Abraham?

Leviticus and Numbers

AFTER THE EXODUS, GOD GATHERS his people around Mount Sinai and gives them numerous laws relating to their life as the people of God. In particular, a great deal of attention is given to the planning and construction of a moveable tabernacle (or tent) in which God will dwell as his people move towards the Promised Land. The tabernacle is a sign of God's deep desire to involve himself with his people and bless them. To have the creator of the universe living amongst them is an extraordinary privilege.

God's laws carry on through Leviticus as Moses teaches the people of Israel how to stand in proper awe of God's mercy and holiness. If Israel is to be a nation with God living within it as king, there are certain matters of 'royal protocol' that must be observed.

In the book of Numbers, the Israelites finally leave Mount Sinai and move to the edge of the Promised Land. They send spies into the Promised Land to help plan the invasion. But things don't go well. The spies bring back stories of fierce inhabitants in the land, and the

Israelites become afraid. Out of fear they refuse to enter the land God has promised them. This is essentially an act of mistrust in God and so, as discipline, Israel is made to wander the desert for 40 years. It is during this period that God miraculously provides for Israel with food, drink and sandals that don't wear out! God is teaching his people that he is faithful and can be relied upon.

At the end of this time, Israel again gathers at the edge of the Promised Land for a second attempt at entering. The book of Deuteronomy is made up of three speeches that Moses gives just before this second attempt.

10. Read Deuteronomy 7:7-10. Why is God doing what he is doing?

11. Read Deuteronomy 6:4-15. What should Israel's response be?

12. Read Deuteronomy 7:1-4. What specific things should Israel do to safeguard their wholehearted allegiance to God?

13. As they prepare to enter the Promised Land, the Israelites need to be reminded that their permanent possession of the land isn't automatic. In fact, in Deuteronomy 29, Moses paints a vivid picture of the possible horrors of exile from the land. He imagines a future where horrified onlookers will ask, "Why has the Lord done this?" If these terrible things actually happened, what would be the answer to this question (Deut 29:25-28)?

14. Moses gives the Israelites a clear choice. Read Deuteronomy 30:15-20. What are Israel's options?

On the edge

WE LEAVE THIS STUDY WITH ISRAEL now poised on the edge of the Promised Land, ready to make their second attempt at entering. As we have noted several times already, Israel is only here by virtue of God's gracious promises to Abraham. God is faithfully keeping his promises to form Abraham's descend-ants into a great nation, bless them and settle them in their own special land. Yet, despite God's generosity, the Israelites have been grumbling and com-plaining every step of the way.

In our next study we'll consider whether things improve once the Israelites actually get into the Promised

Land—and we'll be watching to see how much heed they take of the warnings given by Moses. Before we leave this study however, there are exciting things for us to see about Jesus.

The greatest escape

Before the present Australian Parliament House was built in Canberra, it was possible to visit a model of the proposed building. The model was a beautifully presented miniature, housed in its own special display centre. But as impressive as the model was, its purpose was to point to the final structure. The model had a role to play, but it obviously paled into insignificance alongside the real thing.

That is how Jesus treats the Exodus. The night before his death, as he is celebrating the Passover festival with his disciples, Jesus explains that he has come to fulfil the Passover. In fact, his disciples are to replace the Passover meal with a meal in remembrance of him (Luke 22). In other words, the Exodus may be the greatest escape in the Old Testament— but it is not the greatest escape in the Bible. The Exodus was a prelude, a foreshowing of the rescue that Christ would achieve on the cross. As such, all four characteristics we noted earlier about the Exodus find their fulfilment in a much more radical sense through the death of Jesus, the lamb of God, who died to free us from our slavery.

» Implications

(Choose one or more of the following to think about further or to discuss in your group.)

- Consider how each of these characteristics of the Exodus finds its fulfilment in Christ:

  - A lamb is sacrificed (John 1:29; Rev 5:6-10)

  - God did it (Eph 2:4-9)

- From slavery to freedom (Rom 8:1-4; Gal 5:1-6)

- From poverty to riches (Eph 1:3, 18; 2 Cor 8:9)

- In the book of Hebrews, Israel is presented as an example for us not to follow (Heb 3:7-13). In what specific ways can we encourage each other not to harden our hearts against God?

- Moses urged Israel never to forget the Exodus, since it was the event that gave them their identity. The same is true of the cross for us. What steps can we take to ensure that we never forget the cross? What things can threaten to push our attention away from Christ?

- We've covered quite a lot of material in this study. Is there any one section that you have found particularly interesting or helpful or instructive? Why?

- God's faithfulness rating is still stuck firmly on 10, but the Israelites can be a frustrating bunch! Give them a rating for their faithfulness to God though this study.

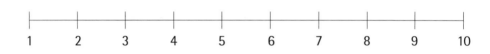

1   2   3   4   5   6   7   8   9   10

» Give thanks and pray

- Thank God for communicating with his people so clearly and carefully.
- Thank God for sending Christ to rescue us from slavery to death through his work on the cross.
- Ask God to keep giving you a better understanding of God's plan for salvation through Jesus, as you study his word.

GREAT EXPECTATIONS

[JOSHUA–1 SAMUEL]

1. Imagine that you're an Israelite living during the time of Deuteronomy. You've been wandering in the desert for 40 years, during which you watched an entire generation die out. Moses is dead and Joshua is your new leader. You are about to cross the Jordan into the land that God promised to Abraham's descendants. How do you feel, and why?

Looking forward to a land

MELISSA'S HANDS TREMBLED with excitement as she sat in the theatre seat. What a night! Other performances had come and gone but she'd never been able to get a seat. Either the tickets had been too expensive or else they had been sold out before she could get one. But this time was different. Melissa had been saving for the ticket for months. She had waited in line for hours for the box office to open so she could get the best seat in the house. Tonight was the big night. The curtain lifted. Melissa's pulse quickened.

Most of us know the feelings of excited anticipation that occur when an event we've been looking forward to finally happens. That's how we should be feeling as the curtain opens on the book of Joshua. The Israelites are finally about to set foot in the Promised Land!

It hasn't always looked as if Israel would get to this point. A powerful Pharaoh opposed their release from slavery. Acts of disobedience resulted in Israel wandering in the desert for 40 years of discipline. Yet through it all, God has been astonishingly faithful to his promises to Abraham. God has made Israel into a numerous people. Now they are poised to take possession of the land that God had promised Abraham. Expectations are great. Let's see how they get on.

2. The book of Joshua details the initial conquests of the Promised Land. Read Joshua 1:1-7.

- Why is God giving them the land?

- What does he expect from the Israelites and Joshua in return?

3. Look up the following verses in Joshua. How are the people responding to God?

- 7:1

- 9:14-15

- 17:12-13

- 18:1-3

- 24:19-24

4. Read Joshua 24:28-33. How does the book of Joshua conclude? What has been achieved so far concerning God's promises?

Joshua

WHEN WE WERE AT SCHOOL, WE learnt about continental drift. Continental drift is the process in which landmasses are slowly moving across the surface of the earth. It's far too slow for us to notice, but it's so powerful that it can cause an entire mountain range to form.

In Joshua we encounter relationship drift, as Israel drifts from God. It's almost too slow to notice at first, but it's happening—and it can have catastrophic results. The book of Joshua has so many positive events in it, as city after city is conquered by the Israelites, that it's possible to miss the signs of relationship drift. But as the book unfolds, the Israelites become more and more apathetic about God. We see this in their failure to totally remove the Canaanites from the land they're moving into, even though God has repeatedly commanded them to do so, promising to give them victory if they follow him.

All this is very disappointing. Joshua started out with great expectations. The Israelites were entering the Promised Land and God had promised to care for them there. It was as if the garden-of-Eden experience was going to happen all over again—God's people in God's place being blessed by God. Sadly, it wasn't working out all that well.

Perhaps things will get better.

5. The book of Judges describes the 'mopping-up operations' in the land of Canaan. There are still plenty of idolatrous and pagan tribes to be driven out. Throughout this time, Israel is unique among the nations because it doesn't have a political king. Instead it is led by 'judges'. Read Judges 2:10-19 and draw a diagram to represent what's happening during this period of history.

6. Read Judges 8:22-23. What do you think is the significance of the fact that the Israelites don't have a human king?

7. Read Judges 3:1-4. What is God doing with his people during this time?

8. What is the result (3:7, 3:12, 4:1, 6:1, 13:1)?

9. What state is Israel in by the end of the book (21:25)?

Judges and 1 Samuel

ISRAEL'S DISOBEDIENCE IS STARTING to gather speed. The Israelites are continually flirting with other gods and compromising their relationship with the true God. Even the judges themselves reflect a steady decline in quality. By the time we meet Samson at the end of the book of Judges, he seems nothing more than an arrogant womanizer who is only interested in saving Israel when it satisfies his love life!

In many ways, Samson provides a picture in miniature of Israel. Just as Samson compromises his allegiance to God by repeatedly seeking after foreign women, Israel compromises her allegiance to God by repeatedly seeking after foreign gods. The signs are not good for Israel. Samson eventually dies as a prisoner at the hands of his enemies. Will the same happen to Israel?

The story continues in the books of 1 and 2 Samuel.

10. Samuel was the last of the judges. Though he was a godly man, his sons weren't. Israel falls into a state of decay. In an attempt to restore matters, the people make an important request in 1 Samuel 8. What do they ask for and why?

11. What is God's response?

12. What does God specifically warn them of?

13. Saul is chosen as the first king of Israel, a choice God promotes so as to teach the Israelites something of the perils of human kingship. But God's real aim is to bless his people, and so in 1 Samuel 16:1-13, God selects the ideal king. Who is it, and why is he an unexpected choice?

14. Read 1 Samuel 31:1-7. What is the condition of Israel by the end of the book?

What's wrong with Israel?

IN THIS STUDY WE HAVE COVERED the main events of Israel's settlement into the Promised Land as described in the books of Joshua, Judges and 1 Samuel. All in all, it's a pretty sorry tale! Israel entered the Promised Land with high hopes, but through repeated sin and rebellion they are now a shattered people at the mercy of the Philistines.

Throughout this segment of their history, the problem with Israel is that they want all the blessings from God but are unprepared for the responsibility that goes with them. Israel refuses to follow God wholeheartedly. They want God's blessings on their own terms, rather than on God's terms. They settle in the land amongst the Canaanites, but allow them to remain rather than removing them as God wanted. The Israelites presume on God's grace, only taking an interest in God when things get difficult and they need help. They even decide to have a king so that they can be like the other nations. All this is a rejection of God as their ruler.

In many ways, this sad period of history is like the Fall all over again. God's people are in God's land, but they are rejecting God's way of life. Adam and Eve were expelled from the garden of Eden for their rebellion. What will the future hold for Israel in the promised land of Canaan?

God's faithfulness

If there is a ray of hope in this gloomy period of Israelite history, it is the way in which God's surprising grace continually shines through. Despite the frustration with human sin, God remains at work. Certainly he uses some rather unexpected people and unexpected weapons, but through it all God consistently works to save Israel from her enemies so as to fulfil his promises. Even when the judge actually dies, as in the case of Samson, God is still powerfully at work saving his people (Judg 16:30).

This is a part of the Old Testament, therefore, which makes us look forward to a new Joshua, a new judge, a new king; to a person who will not fail, but who will conquer the enemies of God once for all—Jesus Christ. In him we'll finally meet the solution to all humanity's problems, and the answer to all God's promises.

» Implications

(Choose one or more of the following to think about further or to discuss in your group.)

• Israel's rejection of God is revealed in her chasing after the gods of the Canaanites. What are the false gods we frequently chase after? What specific things can we do to protect ourselves?

• After all that God had done for them, why do you think the Israelites so quickly deserted him in the Promised Land? What lessons can we learn?

• Read Joshua 1:9. In what way, if any, do these words to Joshua have relevance for us?

- During the period of the judges, God used some unexpected people and weapons to defeat his enemies. How is this also true of Christ?

- As we've seen in this study, Israel's faithfulness to God has been a bit wobbly. How do you think their faithfulness rating is going?

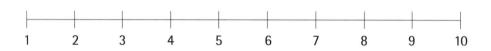

1   2   3   4   5   6   7   8   9   10

» Give thanks and pray

- Pray that you would learn from Israel how *not* to act towards God. Repent of your own sinful disobedience and ask God to help you keep trusting him.
- Thank God for his graciousness in keeping his promises. Praise him for the ultimate answer to all his promises—Jesus.
- Pray that God will open the hearts and minds of people close to you who have rejected Jesus. Ask God to have mercy on them.

THE KINGDOM COMES

[DAVID–SOLOMON]

1. Congratulations! We are now halfway through our studies on the Old Testament. What would you say if a friend asked you, "What's the Old Testament all about?"

2. Think back to what your answer would have been before you started these studies. In what ways is your answer different now?

Wait—there's more!

YOU'VE SEEN THE ADS ON TELEVI- sion. Maybe you've even bought the products. "Wait—there's more! Order this amazing new combination DVD storage rack and orange juicer today, and you'll receive these incredible steak knives at no extra cost. And that's not all…"

Trouble is, when the package arrives in the mail, it's mostly junk. The steak knives are blunt, the orange juice squirts all over your DVD collection, and you finally realize that what you got wasn't nearly as good as what you were promised.

But where God is concerned, his promises never disappoint. So far in our studies, we've been following the fulfilment of God's promises to Abraham. But, as we'll discover in this study, God is not content merely to keep his promises to Abraham. There's more. And it really does get better and better! As it becomes evident that God's promises to Abraham are finally being fulfilled in the land of Israel, God makes new promises to add blessing on top of blessing.

After a time of internal political turmoil in Israel, things have finally settled down. David is king, Jerusalem is his capital city, and he's living in style in a cedar-lined palace. But that's just the start of the good things God has in mind.

Read 2 Samuel 7:1–17.

3. What does David want to build?

4. What does God want to do first?

5. Who has been responsible for David's 'good fortune' so far (vv. 8–9)?

---

6. What does the future hold for David and his family (vv. 9, 11–15)?

7. What does the future hold for Israel (v. 10)?

8. What similarities can you see between the promises God is making to David, and his earlier promises to Abraham?

9. What new features have been added?

10. As usual, we'll need to keep in mind the incredible ability we humans have to mess things up. What small hint of possible future problems do you notice among these promises? (Keep this in mind!)

11. Read David's response to God's words, in verses 18-29. God's new promises are not the cheap and nasty free-steak-knives-thrown-in-with-the-deal type! David is dumbfounded by the sheer magnitude and scope of God's generosity. If someone had asked David to summarize the story of the Old Testament so far, which verses in this section do you think would make up his answer?

David's son

GOD HAS SOME GREAT PLANS FOR David and his family. For starters, he's made the remarkable promise that David's line will rule God's people forever! As a first step, David's son will build the temple David wants to build. The symbol of God's dwelling place with his people will become a permanent focus for the people of Israel. And, most remarkable of all, there will be a special bond between God and Israel's king. "I will be to him a father," says God, "and he shall be to me a son" (2 Sam 7:14a).

Ominously, though, God already anticipates more sin and failure. And when it happens, there will be consequences: "When he commits iniquity, I will discipline him with the rod of men, with the stripes of the sons of men..." (2 Sam 7:14b). Even so, God promises to remain faithful. His love will remain with David's line forever, no matter what.

The next few chapters (2 Samuel 8-10) describe how the Kingdom of Israel is consolidated under David's rule. Surrounding tribes fall like dominoes and become subject to his rule. Tributes and gifts of precious gold and useful bronze flow in from every direction.

But there's a fatal flaw. David commits a big-time sin, and the consequences will haunt his family for generations. A spur-of-the-moment adulterous affair with the beautiful Bathsheba leads to the murder of her innocent husband. The rest of 2 Samuel reads like an episode of a sleazy soap opera, with the royal family of Israel racked by family feuds, rivalry and murderous ambition.

It's brother against brother in an eerie reminder of the relationship between Cain and Abel outside of Eden. Surely life in the Promised Land should be better than this!

For a moment, at least, it is. Surprisingly, Bathsheba—the wife David gained through his deception—gives birth to the son who will bear God's blessing. His name is Solomon, and under his rule Israel enters a golden era of peace and prosperity.

Read 1 Kings 3:1–15.

Sounds promising, doesn't it? Solomon is king—and when God speaks to him in a dream and offers to fulfil his greatest wish, Solomon asks for something far better than a packet of Tim Tams that never runs out. (Haven't seen the ad? Google it!)

12. What hints can you see in verses 6-8 that Solomon has God's long-standing promises in mind?

13. What is Solomon's request?

14. What is God's response?

   • v. 12

   • v. 13

15. Look up the following references and consider which of God's promises is being fulfilled.

- 1 Kings 4:20

- 1 Kings 4:21

- 1 Kings 6:1-3

- 1 Kings 10:4-9

A palace for Solomon, a house for God

IF DAVID'S KINGDOM WAS GLORIOUS, Solomon's was even more glorious. Under Solomon's rule the Promised Land is firmly settled, Israel is elevated to the status of a world power, and even Gentile rulers (such as the Queen of Sheba) praise the God of Israel. It seems that the promises to Abraham have finally come true.

But there's more! God's promises to David also seem to be coming to fulfilment. Solomon becomes the first king of Israel who achieves his rule through birthright. Furthermore, he succeeds in building the temple in Jerusalem to replace the tabernacle as God's symbolic dwelling place in the midst of his people.

But there's even more! Solomon asks God for wisdom, and God says "Yes!" In fact, God gives Solomon the works—

Solomon gets the things he didn't ask for as well, like prosperity and honour!

These are great days, and this mood of excitement is reflected in Solomon's moving prayer at the dedication of the temple in 1 Kings 8—a prayer that points us back to the great covenant promises of God. Take a look, for example, at these words in verses 23 and 24:

> "O Lord, God of Israel, there is no God like you, in heaven above or on earth beneath, keeping covenant and showing steadfast love to your servants who walk before you with all their heart, who have kept with your servant David my father what you declared to him. You spoke with your mouth, and with your hand have fulfilled it this day."

Or how about verse 56?

> "Blessed be the Lord who has given rest to his people Israel, according to all that he promised. Not one word has failed of all his good promise, which he spoke by Moses his servant."

This truly is the golden age of Israel. The big question is, will Solomon practise what he preaches? Is Solomon someone whose heart is "wholly true to the Lord our God" (1 Kgs 8:61)? Scratch the surface, and what sort of king do you find? In the next study, we'll find out. But for now, notice some small, disturbing signs.

Read 1 Kings 6:38–7:1.

16. As well as building the temple, Solomon builds himself an impressive new palace. Which building project took longest?

17. Compare the dimensions of the temple in 1 Kings 6:2 with the dimensions of the palace in 1 Kings 7:2. Which is the more impressive building? What might this reveal about Solomon's priorities?

18. Look back at 1 Kings 3:14. What is the condition attached to God's promise of wisdom?

19. Look further back, to 1 Kings 3:1-4. Are there any hints here that Solomon might have been heading for trouble? List them.

20. Look even further back, at Deuteronomy 17:16-17. Long before Solomon was even a speck on the horizon of history, God had given some very clear guidelines for those who would be kings. What three things are to be especially avoided?

-

-

-

These will serve as useful 'performance indicators' for our new king. Keep them in mind! (We'll come back to them in our next study.)

›› Implications

(Choose one or more of the following to think about further or to discuss in your group.)

- How does Solomon's glorious reign compare with Jesus'? Look up Matthew 12:42, 27:37, 28:18. How was Jesus less glorious? More glorious?

- Under the rule of David and Solomon, the borders of Israel grew to encompass the small surrounding nations. What is the scope of the rule of King Jesus?

- In practical terms, what does it mean that Jesus has this authority over you?

- What does Jesus call his disciples to do in the light of this great authority that has been given to him through his death and resurrection (Matt 28:19)?

- God has done a great job of keeping his promises: David and Solomon have both said so in their own words. And, in spite of a few stumbles, David and Solomon have been holding things together pretty well, too. As they're the main representatives of Israel we've looked at in this study, give Israel a faithfulness rating based on the performance of their kings.

1   2   3   4   5   6   7   8   9   10

» Give thanks and pray

- Give thanks for our ruling king—Jesus. Ask God to help you submit to Jesus as lord of your life, and give up your hold on the reins.
- Keep thanking God for being true to his promises. Pray that you would never tire of praising him for his faithfulness.
- Ask God to give you a godly and right attitude towards the earthly ruler/s whom God has appointed over your country.

»STUDY 6

THE KINGDOM GOES

[SOLOMON-EXILE]

1. Think about your own experiences of life. Do you tend to forget about God when things are going well or when things are going poorly? Why is that?

Going up, coming down

"WHAT GOES UP MUST COME down!" This is true of many things—aeroplanes, Frisbees, umbrellas, socks. Unfortunately it is also true of King Solomon.

In our last study, we examined King Solomon on his way up. Israel is having economic and military success, and is growing in cultural sophistication. People want to go to Israel for their holidays. Money is pouring into the country because businesses want to invest in

Israel. All the rulers of the world are lining up to have their photo taken with King Solomon of Israel. Solomon is *TIME* magazine's 'Man of the Year'. And it looks as if all the promises God has ever made have finally come true.

God promised Abraham that he would make his descendants into a great nation and bless them in their own land. Under Solomon, it seems as if it has all finally happened. In 2 Samuel 7, God promised King David that his family would rule over his people forever. Under Solomon, it seems as if that promise has also been fulfilled. This is the golden age of Israel.

But what goes up usually comes down. King Solomon goes up like a skyrocket and comes down like a lead weight.

2. Think back to the three key indicators for kingship that we discovered in Deuteronomy 17. (We looked at them in the last study.) Let's see how Solomon fares...

STRIKE 1
Read 1 Kings 10:26 and 28. What has Solomon forgotten?

STRIKE 2
Read 1 Kings 10:27. What has Solomon forgotten?

STRIKE 3
Read 1 Kings 11:1-8. What has Solomon forgotten?

3. What does God promise to do as punishment (11:9-13)?

4. Read 1 Kings 12:1-24. What are the political reasons for the splitting apart of Israel? What are the underlying spiritual reasons?

The bubble bursts

EVEN IN OUR LAST STUDY, WE NOTED several aspects about David and Solomon that made us suspicious of how firm Israel's faithfulness was. In 1 Kings 10-11, however, it becomes clear that Israel and her rulers are far from being as faithful as they should be. In spite of the fact that God has spoken to Solomon in person, and spelled out his requirements in his law, Solomon has chosen the path of unfaithfulness. He starts to hoard gold and he gathers chariots and horses, putting his confidence in the might of his army rather than the might of God. And worst of all, Solomon marries foreign women who lead his heart away from God. Solomon is repeating the very same sin that has been Israel's downfall all along. Despite God's command, Israel has consistently refused to follow him wholeheartedly.

The consequences are disastrous! From here on, the books of 1 and 2 Kings trace the decline of the once great kingdom of Israel.

Let's take it step by step. After Solomon's son Rehoboam takes the throne, there's a civil war. The northern tribes rebel and the nation of Israel splits into two halves. The northern section retains the name Israel, elects a new king named Jeroboam (who is not from the family of David), and sets up a new capital at Samaria. Jeroboam also establishes altars at Dan and Bethel and urges the people to worship there rather than at the temple in Jerusalem.

The southern tribe of Judah retains

David's family as its rulers, remains with Jerusalem as its capital city, and keeps the temple. But things are never the same. The golden age of Israel is now well and truly over.

The rest of 1 and 2 Kings describes the separate fates of the northern and southern kingdoms. It can all get a bit confusing as we jump from one kingdom to the other, but for the moment let's just stick with the story of the northern kingdom.

5. How do the kings of Israel seem to be going?

- 1 Kings 15:25-26

- 1 Kings 15:33-34

- 1 Kings 16:29-33

- 1 Kings 22:51-53

6. Much of 1 and 2 Kings is devoted to the ministry of the prophets Elijah and Elisha. Both these men warned the people of Israel (the northern kingdom) about the consequences of rejecting God's law. Read 1 Kings 19:10. What is Elijah's assessment of how things are going?

7. Amos and Hosea were two prophets who also called Israel to repentance. Read Hosea 4:1-3. How does Hosea think Israel is going?

8. Read 2 Kings 17:1-23. What happens to Israel and why?

Israel: the northern kingdom

THE HISTORY OF THE NORTHERN kingdom is a sorry tale indeed. Its first king, Jeroboam, sets the pattern. Not only did Jeroboam reject God's word by becoming king in the first place (he wasn't a descendant of David), but he also rejected God's temple in Jerusalem and led the people to worship idols. All the other kings followed in Jeroboam's footsteps, and Israel sank into a pit of immorality and apostasy. Under God's judgement, Israel was eventually crushed by the Assyrian Empire, and the northern kingdom disappeared from the pages of history.

Maybe things are going better in the southern kingdom…

9. What are the kings of Judah like? Here's a sample:

- 2 Kings 8:16-19

- 2 Kings 16:1-4

- 2 Kings 18:1-4

- 2 Kings 21:1-6

(Still not sure? Then also have a look at 2 Kings 12:1-3, 15:1-4, 21:19-22, 22:1-2, 23:31-32.)

10. Jeremiah was one of the prophets who brought God's message to Judah. Read Jeremiah 11:1-13. What is Jeremiah's message and what is it based on?

11. Read 2 Kings 25:1-26. What happens to Judah?

12. How are God's promises to Abraham going by the end of 2 Kings?

Judah: the southern kingdom

DESPITE RETAINING KINGS FROM David's family and centering their worship at the temple in Jerusalem, the southern kingdom also degenerates into rebellion against God. Although some of the kings, like Josiah, try to turn the people's heart back to God, they are unsuccessful. Even warnings from prophets like Isaiah, Jeremiah and Ezekiel aren't enough. Judah continually falls victim to the same sin as Solomon—they turn their hearts to other gods and they are not fully devoted to the Lord their God.

Way back in Deuteronomy, God had warned his people of what would happen if they deserted him (Deut 28:15-68). God said that he would punish them by driving them out of the Promised Land. They would be enslaved in a foreign land. And that's exactly what happened.

In the event known as 'the Exile', Judah was conquered by the Babylonian Empire. Jerusalem was destroyed, the temple was levelled and thousands of prisoners were taken back to Babylon as exiles. (Daniel is an example of one such exile.)

By the end of 2 Kings, 'Israel' is in an utter shambles. Idolatry and immorality has been punished with civil war and conquest. In the space of 27 chapters, 'Israel' has gone from the heights of their golden age under Solomon to the gloomy depths of the Exile.

Is this the end for 'Israel'? What of God's promises? Stay tuned for the next study.

The kings are dead, long live the King

If you visit a jeweller and ask to look at some diamonds, more often than not the jeweller will show you the diamonds against a black velvet cloth. The dark background is useful because it serves to emphasize the brightness and beauty of the diamond. That's what the books of 1 and 2 Kings do for Jesus Christ. The gloom and darkness of Israel's sinful kings serve to highlight the beauty of Christ's kingship.

Most of Israel's kings were selfish, evil leaders who led the people away from the true and living God. In the words of Ezekiel, they were like harsh and brutal shepherds who cared nothing for the sheep (Ezekiel 34). Jesus, however, is the good shepherd who properly cares for his flock (John 10). Jesus leads with self-sacrificing love—a love that even takes him to the cross.

For those of us who live this side of the cross, then, even this depressing period of Israel's history has an exciting dimension to it. As we see Israel's kings at their worst, it forces us to look forward to a more satisfying fulfilment of God's promises to Abraham.

» Implications

(Choose one or more of the following to think about further or to discuss in your group.)

- If Solomon was so wise, how could he go so wrong? Are there any warnings here for us?

- Throughout this period of history, Israel and her kings refuse to be God's holy people. As followers of Jesus, we also are called to be holy (1 Pet 1:13-16).

  - What does this mean in practical terms?

  - How are you going at this? Is there any real difference between your life and attitudes and those of your non-Christian friends? Why, or why not?

  - Throughout this period of history, are there any kings who really stick in your mind? Why?

- Have you ever doubted that Jesus is a good leader? Why?

» Give thanks and pray

- Ask God to raise up Christian leaders for our countries, and pray that these leaders will support the spread of the gospel. Give thanks to God for revealing to us that he (not man) is in control of the world.
- Pray that the leaders of our churches, both in your own country and abroad, would not be corrupted by power and wealth.
- Ask God to help you, as you strive to be holy, to remain wholly devoted to him. Ask him to transform you so that your life will be starkly different from the lives of the non-Christians around you.

IS GOD DEAD?

[THE EXILE]

1. The words 'Exodus' and 'Exile' appear to be quite similar. The events are very different! From what you already know of the Exile (see previous study), list as many differences as you can between the events of the Exodus and the Exile.

An absent God?

IN THE MID 1960S, AMERICA'S
TIME magazine ran a famous headline.
It was a period of history when America
was gripped by the fear of communism
and the threat of nuclear war. Social
unrest was spreading like a cancer as
political and racial riots erupted
throughout the country. Martin Luther
King Jr had been assassinated in Memphis. President John F Kennedy had
been assassinated in Dallas. Senator
Robert F Kennedy had been assassinated
in Los Angeles.

In the midst of all this national distress, TIME magazine was published
with a black cover containing three simple words in red... "Is God Dead?" It
seemed the obvious question to ask. If
God was there, then why wasn't he doing
something? Why was the world in such
a mess? Didn't God care? Was he dead?

In this study we enter a time of
Israel's history when questions like these
were on the lips of every Israelite.

2. Lamentations is a book written at the time of the Exile. Read chapter 1. What reasons does it give for the Exile?

3. What emotional effect did the Exile have on the people of Judah? Why do you think it had such a big impact?

4. Read Lamentations 3:19-33. In the midst of great despair, what is the writer's basis for hope?

By the waters of Babylon we wept

As we discovered in study 6, Judah has been punished for her sinfulness by being conquered by the Babylonian Empire. Jerusalem and the temple have been destroyed, thousands of prisoners have been dragged back to Babylon to live as exiles, and the Israelites are in utter despair and confusion.

How could God do something like this? What about all God's promises to Abraham—promises that Israel would be a blessed nation in her own land? Now the Israelites are exiles in a foreign land. It's a complete disaster. The only other Old Testament event to rival the tragedy of the Exile is the Fall, when Adam and Eve rebelled in the garden of Eden. Indeed, there are strong similarities between the Fall and the Exile. In both cases, God's special people rebel against his rule and are thrown out of their special land as punishment. History is repeating itself—sin has again reared its ugly head.

The big question is: Has God totally given up on Israel, or does he plan to restore her? The answer can be found in the words of the prophets who proclaim God's word in the time leading up to the Exile, and even continuing through it. Among these prophets are Jeremiah, Ezekiel and Isaiah.

5. According to the prophets, what will happen after the Exile?

- Jeremiah 29:10-14

- Jeremiah 16:14-15

- Jeremiah 31:31-34

- Ezekiel 37:21-28

- Ezekiel 36:33-36

- Isaiah 65:17-25

6. Within these future plans for God's people, two specific individuals will play an important role. Who are they and what do they do?

- Person 1: Jeremiah 33:14-26 and Isaiah 11:1-5

- Person 2: Isaiah 52:13-53:12

A brave new world

DESPITE THE GLOOM OF THE EXILE, the prophets never gave up hope for a future fulfilment of God's promises to Abraham and King David. Indeed, the grandeur of what God was to do after the Exile would make everything that came before pale into insignificance. Israel was going to enjoy a rescue from Babylon that would surpass even the Exodus (Jer 16:14-15). A new covenant would now be established in which sin would be forgiven—and, best of all, God would give his people new hearts in which they would actually desire to do good (Jeremiah 31).

These are majestic promises! Through his prophets God has recommitted himself to break sin's stranglehold on humanity. The result will be new heavens and a new earth in which the harmony and peace of the garden of Eden will be recaptured (Isa 65:17-25).

Within this new creation, two specific individuals will play very significant roles. The first is a new Davidic king, who will rule his people in righteousness and justice. The second is a mysterious servant, whose suffering will somehow lead to the forgiveness of sins. We'll have more to say about these two people later, but for now let's investigate what practical implications these promises have for the exiles in captivity.

7. Read Jeremiah 29:1-9. How should the exiles respond to the Exile?

8. Read Jeremiah 29:10-11. Why do you think this advice in verses 1-9 is given?

9. Read Daniel 3. What lessons do you see here about how the exiles are to live in Babylon?

10. Read Daniel 9:1-19. According to Daniel, how should the exiles now respond to God?

11. What signs of comfort can be seen in the experiences of Daniel and his colleagues?

Aliens in a foreign land

WHILE IN EXILE, THE PROPHETS encouraged the Israelites to repent and return to God. It was Israel's blatant sinfulness that led God to cause the Exile; it was a painful but necessary disciplinary event. The appropriate response, then, was to learn from the discipline and renew their devotion to God. Israel was therefore called on to settle into normal life in Babylon—but never in such a way as to compromise their commitment to God.

The words of the prophets and the example of people like Daniel and his friends encouraged the Israelites to repent and once again live the life of faith. They were to look beyond their present circumstances, trust in God's word for the future, and therefore refuse to compromise on following God. This was exactly the same lifestyle the Israelites had been taught to live in the wilderness (study 3) but which they had failed in dismally during their occupancy of the Promised Land (study 6). The question remains as to whether the Exile experience will teach the Israelites to learn from their mistakes.

The servant king

In study 2 we noted that Jesus Christ is the ultimate fulfilment of all of God's promises (2 Cor 1:20). The prophetic promises we have investigated in this study are no exception.

Christ ushers in the new covenant through his death on the cross (Luke 22:20). By his death, Jesus secures forgiveness of sins and enables a deep relationship with God in which his Spirit transforms and shapes our hearts (Rom 8:1-4; Gal 5:16-26).

As we've discovered in this study, the new Davidic king and the suffering servant of God both seem to have a key role in establishing the new covenant—a king who will rule God's people with righteousness, and a servant who will somehow provide for the forgiveness of sins. The genius of God is that Jesus Christ fulfils *both* of these roles. Jesus appears as the Messiah, the divinely anointed ruler of God's people. Yet Jesus is a king who rules his people by serving them. He went to the cross to suffer in our place. Our servant king was indeed "wounded for our transgressions" and "crushed for our iniquities" (Isa 53:5).

» Implications

(Choose one or more of the following to think about further or to discuss in your group.)

- The modern Christian's position is quite similar to that of the exiles in Babylon. We are aliens in a land that is not our ultimate home. How does the promise of our heavenly home help us deal with life? (See Romans 8:18-39 and 2 Thessalonians 1:5-10.)

- What pressures do we face to compromise our faith in Christ?

- What words of advice does 1 Peter 2:11-12 have to offer? What specific things can we do to put these verses into practice?

- Christ is both the anointed Messiah and suffering servant of God. How do these two aspects of Christ's role spur us on to greater obedience?

- Recall a time when things have not gone well for you.
  - What sorts of thoughts did you have?

  - How did you feel towards God?

- Does Israel's experience of the Exile provide any lessons about God that might help us deal with such times?

- Is God still being faithful to his promises? Update his rating.

- Things haven't gone well for the people of Israel. They're paying the consequences for their unfaithfulness. But maybe they've learned their lesson? Maybe you've seen some signs of progress? Maybe they've turned the corner? Update Israel's faithfulness rating to reflect your opinion on their current state.

- How would you rate your own faithfulness to God?

» Give thanks and pray

- Thank God for his sovereign control over everything. Thank God also for the comfort and reassurance it is to know that he has a good plan for his people.
- Ask God to help you continue to trust in his sovereignty.
- Thank God for the hope we see in Lamentations, in which we also share: "The steadfast love of the Lord never ceases; his mercies never come to an end; they are new every morning".
- Using 1 Peter 2:11-12, pray for yourself and those in your church and Bible study groups.

A DIARY OF DISASTER

[NEHEMIAH]

1. Look back to the timeline you created at the start of this book (p. 9). How accurate was your picture of the Old Testament? What events were at the end of your timeline?

Happy endings

MOVIES DON'T ALWAYS HAVE happy endings. Have you ever seen *Butch Cassidy and the Sundance Kid*? You might remember it as the film that made stars of Robert Redford and Paul Newman; you may remember it as the film that made a hit of the song 'Raindrops Keep Falling on my Head'. But most probably, you'll remember it for the devastating ending. Our likeable cowboy heroes are actually villains, and they're finally surrounded by hundreds of soldiers and lawmen. Butch and Sundance storm out of their hiding place to face overwhelming odds. A volley of shots rings out. And the credits roll down the screen.

A memorable ending? Yes. A happy ending? No.

It's exactly the same with the Old Testament. Though there have been high points, though there have been hopeful signs, though God's faithfulness has been unquestionable, the human heroes have always had a fatal flaw. And in the end, it's a flaw that brings disaster.

The books of Ezra and Nehemiah record the final phases of Old Testament history. Along with other prophets like Zechariah and Malachi, these books describe Israel's resettlement in the Promised Land after the terrible Babylonian exile.

In this study we'll be focusing mainly on Nehemiah. In your spare time, you might like to read through Ezra for additional background.

Read Nehemiah 1.

2. What does chapter 1 tell you about the historical setting of the book?

3. As we've worked through the Old Testament, we've often been reminded about the significance of God's promises to Abraham. What does Nehemiah say about this 'covenant'?

4. Nehemiah quotes from Deuteronomy 30:4-10. What promises has God made in that passage for the specific situation Israel is now in?

5. What questions does this raise about Israel's future in the land?

Rebuilding the wall

AS WE HAVE DISCOVERED, NEHEMIAH is a high-ranking official in the court of the Persian king (1:11). On hearing the news that the rebuilding of Jerusalem is not going well, Nehemiah is driven to prayer.

In chapter 2, Nehemiah gains the king's blessing to return to Jerusalem and help supervise the rebuilding project. Under his leadership, the huge project of rebuilding the city walls is soon under way—a task that dominates most of the book. Why does the city need walls? Naturally, it's to keep out the surrounding enemies; but more than that, perhaps it's a symbol of a boundary marking out the people of God from the peoples round about.

For Nehemiah, at least, the walls are a concrete reminder of God's covenant promises to Abraham—the promise that the land of Israel and the city of Jerusalem will be the impregnable home of God's faithful people. "If the people repent, I'll bring them back to the land and bless them", said God. And Nehemiah is taking God's promise seriously.

After 52 days of hard work, the walls of Jerusalem are finally completed. By the end of chapter 7, God's people are secure in the Promised Land, each in their own town. God's promise to restore his people has been fulfilled. But the question remains—will the newly settled people of Israel be as faithful to God as God has been to them?

Read Nehemiah 9.

6. In Nehemiah 9, the Levites lead a public assembly in prayer. They recount the whole sorry tale of God's covenant blessing and Israel's repeated unfaithfulness. Hopefully, the events mentioned are familiar to you by now! Work through the history detailed in the Levites' prayer and fill in the verse numbers that mark out each section.

   • Creation: verses _____ to _____

   • The promises to Abraham: verses _____ to _____

   • The exodus from Egypt: verses _____ to _____

   • The Law given on Mount Sinai: verses _____ to _____

7. What happened next (vv. 16-17)?

8. How did God respond?

   • Wandering in the desert: verses _____ to _____

   • Taking the Promised Land: verses _____ to _____

9. What happened next (vv. 26-27)?

10. How did God respond when they repented (v. 27)?

11. Verse 28 summarizes the whole routine. How many times does this happen?

12. Why didn't God put an end to the stiff-necked Israelites (v. 31)?

Read Nehemiah 10:28–39.

13. The people of Israel are obviously cut to the heart by the account of the sins of their forefathers. As they call out to God to save them once more from their bondage (remember, they're still under foreign control), they decide to make a binding contract with God (9:38). What do the Israelites now promise (10:29)? List the three key issues this will involve:

- 10:30

- 10:31

- 10:32-39

Rebuilding their holiness

THINGS ARE LOOKING PROMISING. The new walls are dedicated in a glorious celebration that recalls the golden age of King David. (Notice how often his name is mentioned in 12:27-47!) The temple storerooms are full to overflowing. What's more, the Israelites have promised that they will again become the holy and unique people God intended them to be, obeying all his laws and statutes.

It certainly seems that things are finally sorting themselves out. The high expectations of the prophets (see study 7) seem to be well founded. By this time—after 12 years of hard work—Nehemiah figures it's safe to take a trip back to Babylon to report to the king. He spends some time there, and then makes the long trip back to Jerusalem. You'll never guess what he discovers when he returns!

Read Nehemiah 13.

14. What has happened in Nehemiah's absence?

- vv. 10-11

- vv. 15-16

- vv. 23-24

15. How does Nehemiah react (vv. 11, 17-22, 25-28)?

Sleeping with the enemy

AFTER BUILDING THE WALL AND struggling to re-establish a faithful Israel, all Nehemiah's efforts are laid to ruin by the absolute inability of the people of Israel to keep God's covenant. Yes, the city walls have been rebuilt—but the city's people haven't. Nehemiah gave it his best shot, but in the end his diary is a diary of disaster! And so the account of the history of Israel ends on a dismal note indeed, with Israel having stepped right into the same sins as Solomon (vv. 26-27). Nehemiah is left begging God for a pardon (vv. 14, 22, 31).

The Old Testament closes not with a bang, but a whimper.

The Old Testament and Jesus Christ

In a very real sense, therefore, the Exile does not end in the Old Testament (Luke 2:25). Despite Nehemiah's best efforts, the promises of a new exodus, a new creation and a new covenant (study 7) are not achieved. The disappointment is great. But for us, living this side of the cross, the excitement is also great because we are now in a position to appreciate the way in which the entire Old Testament points us towards and prepares us for Jesus Christ. For it is precisely in the disappointment of the Old Testament that we discover our need for Christ.

The great tragedy of the Old Testament is that although there is nothing God wants more than to gather a people to himself, humanity keeps pushing him away. The rebellion started with Adam and Eve at the Fall, and it has persisted all through the Old Testament as the Israelites and their kings simply don't want to be the unique nation God has called them to be. Rather than maintain their national distinctiveness—holiness—they play 'mix-and-match' with the surrounding nations.

The Old Testament therefore points us to the need for God to do something definitive about sin. If God is ever going to be able to reverse the Fall and keep his promises to Abraham, sin has to be dealt with once and for all. It is with this thought in mind that the curtains of the New Testament open and Jesus Christ steps into history. The Son of God himself comes to deal decisively with sin. By dying in our place on the cross, Jesus takes the punishment we deserve. We are given a fresh start.

What's more, we're given a fresh *heart*. Through God's spirit, our lives are changed so that we actually want to do his will in a way that the Israelites could never experience. That's not to say that our obedience to God is automatic—until we reach perfection in heaven, it's still a struggle. And yet we have the resources we need to meet the challenge.

In Christ, therefore, all the promises of God are fulfilled. As God promised Abraham, a blessed people of God are gathered together (1 Pet 2:9-10). As God promised David, one of David's descendants will rule forever in justice and righteousness (Acts 2:29-36). As God promised through the prophets, a new covenant is established (Luke 22:20).

How much Nehemiah would have loved to know the blessings that we enjoy through Christ!

» Implications

(Choose one or more of the following to think about further or to discuss in your group.)

- Why was it so important that the Israelites didn't intermarry with other nations? What application can you see for this principle today? What often happens when this advice is ignored (cf. 2 Cor 6:14)?

- Read Hebrews 8:6-13 and Hebrews 9:15.

    - What is the problem with the old covenant (8:8)?

    - What did God promise to do (8:8b)?

- In what way is the new covenant different (8:10)?

- There's one other key part of the package deal too. What is it (8:12)?

- How does Christ's death make this possible (9:15)?

- How do *you* take part in this new covenant?

- As a follower of Jesus, do you see evidence of the fact that God's law is written on your heart? How?

- If God's people in the Old Testament were called to be unique, even though their laws were only written on stone, what about *us*?

- Congratulations, you made it through the Old Testament! We've followed the saga of Israel from start to finish. Have any sections particularly challenged or comforted you? Why?

- From what you have discovered of God throughout these studies give God a rating for his faithfulness to *you*.

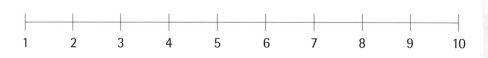

1   2   3   4   5   6   7   8   9   10

- Now give yourself a rating for your present faithfulness to God. What specific things can you be doing to improve on this rating?

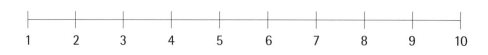

1   2   3   4   5   6   7   8   9   10

» Give thanks and pray

- Thank God for his patience with the Israelites and with us.
- Thank God for the example of Nehemiah—for his faithful attitude towards prayer and God's word, and his real concern for the sinful Israelites.
- Give thanks for the precious gift of the Holy Spirit, who is transforming our hearts and guiding us towards righteousness.
- Praise God for fulfilling all his promises to his people!

APPENDIX

» TIPS FOR LEADERS

Studying the Old Testament

M OST PEOPLE, IF THEY USE the Old Testament at all, treat it like a phonebook or a dictionary—a proof text here, a half-remembered verse there, and the occasional riveting yarn about Noah or Samson or King David thrown in for good measure. But how does it all fit together?

The first step to appreciating the Old Testament is to understand that it contains a single unified story. It is the unfolding story of God's commitment to his promises to bless the world through the descendants of Abraham. The Old Testament is full of promise—and the promise is ultimately fulfilled in Jesus Christ.

Like any other piece of unified literature, the whole Old Testament therefore needs to be read in such a way that recurring themes and patterns are noticed and appreciated. That's what we hope to achieve through these studies. Large slabs of the Old Testament are dealt with so as to draw out the key themes and ideas. Indeed, this is a good way to read any part of the Bible. For example, to truly appreciate each of the Gospels or any of the apostle Paul's letters, they are best read in one sitting. Approaching the Bible in this way helps us to see the 'big picture'.

Dipping into the Old Testament without understanding the big picture can lead to all sorts of problems. We end up with a fragmented understanding of the Old Testament and we never come to grips with the idea that from the beginning of Genesis to the end of Nehemiah—the last stage in the account of Israel's history—it's a story that's going somewhere. As Christians, we especially need to be always ready to jump into the storyline and follow it through to the logical destination—fulfilment in the life, death, resurrection, ascension and kingly rule of Jesus Christ.

Because these studies are designed to highlight the overarching storyline (or framework) of the Old Testament, that means certain issues and events are not even mentioned. Try to avoid the temptation to add bits that you feel should have been included— we've worked hard to slim things down to a manageable outline. And if your group can catch hold of the framework now, you'll find that detailed study of parts of the Old Testament later on will be much easier. Knowing where things fit in the big picture is a huge help in making sense of the Bible. So for now, be content with our 'aerial view', and don't be tempted to get any closer!

Even with our best efforts to make the studies containable, they're still a little more detailed than we would have liked. These studies will work best if your group prepares during the week. Not preparing ahead will mean that the group is very unlikely to be able to complete a study in a single session.

Getting a hold on the sweep of the Old Testament story is exciting. You'll marvel at the way the plot-line fits together. You'll groan at the constant failings of Israel. And most of all, you'll be thrilled at the way all the promises of God find their fulfilment in Christ.

Bryson Smith and Phil Campbell

Feedback on this resource

We really appreciate getting feedback about our resources—not just suggestions for how to improve them, but also positive feedback and ways they can be used. We especially love to hear that the resources may have helped someone in their Christian growth.

You can send feedback to us via the 'Feedback' menu in our online store, or write to us at PO Box 225, Kingsford NSW 2032, Australia.

Matthias Media is an evangelical publishing ministry that seeks to persuade all Christians of the truth of God's purposes in Jesus Christ as revealed in the Bible, and equip them with high-quality resources, so that by the work of the Holy Spirit they will:

- abandon their lives to the honour and service of Christ in daily holiness and decision-making
- pray constantly in Christ's name for the fruitfulness and growth of his gospel
- speak the Bible's life-changing word whenever and however they can— in the home, in the world and in the fellowship of his people.

It was in 1988 that we first started pursuing this mission, and in God's kindness we now have more than 300 different ministry resources being used all over the world. These resources range from Bible studies and books through to training courses and audio sermons.

To find out more about our large range of very useful resources, and to access samples and free downloads, visit our website:

www.matthiasmedia.com

How to buy our resources

1. Direct from us over the internet:
   – in the US: www.matthiasmedia.com
   – in Australia and the rest of the world: www.matthiasmedia.com.au

2. Direct from us by phone:
   – in the US: 1 866 407 4530
   – in Australia: 1300 051 220
   – international: +61 2 9233 4627

> Register at our website for our **free** regular email update to receive information about the latest new resources, **exclusive special offers**, and free articles to help you grow in your Christian life and ministry.

3. Through a range of outlets in various parts of the world. Visit **www.matthiasmedia.com/contact** for details about recommended retailers in your part of the world, including www.thegoodbook.co.uk in the United Kingdom.

4. Trade enquiries can be addressed to:
   – in the US and Canada: sales@matthiasmedia.com
   – in Australia and the rest of the world: sales@matthiasmedia.com.au

Other Interactive and Topical Bible Studies from Matthias Media

Our Interactive Bible Studies (IBS) and Topical Bible Studies (TBS) are a valuable resource to help you keep feeding from God's word. The IBS series works through passages and books of the Bible; the TBS series pulls together the Bible's teaching on topics such as money or prayer. As at May 2012, the series contains the following titles:

Beyond Eden
GENESIS 1-11
Authors: Phillip Jensen and Tony Payne, 9 studies

Out of Darkness
EXODUS 1-18
Author: Andrew Reid, 8 studies

The Shadow of Glory
EXODUS 19-40
Author: Andrew Reid, 7 studies

The One and Only
DEUTERONOMY
Author: Bryson Smith, 8 studies

The Good, the Bad and the Ugly
JUDGES
Author: Mark Baddeley, 10 studies

Famine and Fortune
RUTH
Authors: Barry Webb and David Höhne, 4 studies

Renovator's Dream
NEHEMIAH
Authors: Phil Campbell and Greg Clarke, 7 studies

The Eye of the Storm
JOB
Author: Bryson Smith, 6 studies

The Beginning of Wisdom
PROVERBS VOLUME 1
Author: Joshua Ng, 7 studies

Living the Good Life
PROVERBS VOLUME 2
Author: Joshua Ng, 8 studies

The Search for Meaning
ECCLESIASTES
Author: Tim McMahon, 9 studies

Two Cities
ISAIAH
Authors: Andrew Reid and Karen Morris, 9 studies

Kingdom of Dreams
DANIEL
Authors: Andrew Reid and Karen Morris, 9 studies

Burning Desire
OBADIAH AND MALACHI
Authors: Phillip Jensen and Richard Pulley, 6 studies

Warning Signs
JONAH
Author: Andrew Reid, 6 studies

On That Day
ZECHARIAH
Author: Tim McMahon, 8 studies

Full of Promise
THE BIG PICTURE OF THE O.T.
Authors: Phil Campbell and Bryson Smith, 8 studies

The Good Living Guide
MATTHEW 5:1-12
Authors: Phillip Jensen and Tony Payne, 9 studies

News of the Hour
MARK
Authors: Peter Bolt and Tony Payne, 10 studies

Proclaiming the Risen Lord
LUKE 24-ACTS 2
Author: Peter Bolt, 6 studies

Mission Unstoppable
ACTS
Author: Bryson Smith, 10 studies

The Free Gift of Life
ROMANS 1-5
Author: Gordon Cheng, 8 studies

The Free Gift of Sonship
ROMANS 6-11
Author: Gordon Cheng, 8 studies

The Freedom of Christian Living
ROMANS 12-16
Author: Gordon Cheng, 7 studies

Free for All
GALATIANS
Authors: Phillip Jensen and Kel Richards, 8 studies

Walk this Way
EPHESIANS
Author: Bryson Smith, 8 studies

Partners for Life
PHILIPPIANS
Author: Tim Thorburn, 8 studies

The Complete Christian
COLOSSIANS
Authors: Phillip Jensen and Tony Payne, 8 studies

To the Householder
1 TIMOTHY
Authors: Phillip Jensen and Greg Clarke, 9 studies

Run the Race
2 TIMOTHY
Author: Bryson Smith, 6 studies

The Path to Godliness
TITUS
Authors: Phillip Jensen and Tony Payne, 7 studies

From Shadow to Reality
HEBREWS
Author: Joshua Ng, 10 studies

The Implanted Word
JAMES
Authors: Phillip Jensen and Kirsten Birkett, 8 studies

Homeward Bound
1 PETER
Authors: Phillip Jensen and Tony Payne, 10 studies

All You Need to Know
2 PETER
Author: Bryson Smith, 6 studies

The Vision Statement
REVELATION
Author: Greg Clarke, 9 studies

Bold I Approach
PRAYER
Author: Tony Payne, 6 studies

Cash Values
MONEY
Author: Tony Payne, 5 studies

Sing for Joy
SINGING IN CHURCH
Author: Nathan Lovell, 6 studies

The Blueprint
DOCTRINE
Authors: Phillip Jensen and Tony Payne, 9 studies

Woman of God
THE BIBLE ON WOMEN
Author: Terry Blowes, 8 studies